The BD H
for Lawyers
Part One

Prospects to
Advocates

Tony Reiss, Founding Principal,
Sherwood PSF Consulting

A Bright Pen Book

Text Copyright © Tony Reiss 2011

Cover design by Tony Reiss and James Fitt ©

British Library Cataloguing Publication Data.

A catalogue record for this book is available from the British Library

ISBN 978-0-7552-1399-3

Authors OnLine Ltd
19 The Cinques
Gamlingay, Sandy
Bedfordshire SG19 3NU
England

This book is also available in e-book format, details of which are available at www.authorsonline.co.uk

Tony has had the pleasure of working with many of the leading international firms on BD and related programmes. This is what people have said about Tony's BD coaching:

Absolutely fabulous programme! A particular 'hat tip' to Tony Reiss who I thought was great! I tried one of the models the week after with a Chief Exec and it worked like a dream! I've already been asked to do more work.

> *I've been on loads and loads of courses, and this one stands out as the one I've learned from most. I really liked the personal coaching and how Tony built my self-confidence .*

I'd heard lots of good things and wasn't disappointed. Best course I ever attended was on snow-boarding. This one was as good!

> *The workshop was excellent. The most interaction I have ever experienced.*

Tony – you have inspired me more than any other person I've worked with. I wish you were my boss.

> *I thought the course was extremely useful on both technical and motivational grounds. I suspect that it pays for itself many times over as it acts as a real spur to develop new clients and cement existing relationships.*

You took me out of my comfort zone and I got the benefit out of that. It's different now back in the office.

> *You gave me the confidence and positive feedback that I needed to make the change and go out and do something about it. So I start a new chapter tomorrow, one that I am excited and scared about in equal measure.*

Tony- your enthusiasm, knowledge, experience and brilliant presentations and facilitation skills made it easy for me to listen and learn from you.

> *Tony is lovely, engaging and inclusive. He has such great simple stories and I love the metaphors.*

Purpose of this handbook

Law firms are facing much tougher market conditions. There is evidence that there has been a paradigm shift in the relationship between clients and firms, with clients having much more power and being more assertive. So firms need a new and effective way of structuring their approach to business development (BD).

This Handbook offers such a new approach. One which is based on twenty years of experience working with thirty of the top fifty law firms as well as two of the Big 4 Accounting firms. I have delivered more than 100 courses on BD and coached more than 100 partners and senior associates, so I know it works.

Prospects to Advocates will help practitioners – lawyers – to learn how to be more effective at BD. You don't have to read all of it from start to finish. Each chapter makes sense on its own. Much of it will seem common sense, but I can assure you it isn't common practice!

Some of the content has already appeared in various publications, though much of it is new and based on my training and coaching material.

Prospects to Advocates provides a disciplined, pragmatic framework with guides and checklists to offer practical help. It is designed to keep as a handy reference guide in your desk drawer in case your BD team are busy or if you feel you need some extra help or a second opinion. The emphasis is less on the theory (though there is some) and more on the practicalities of doing BD.

I'm confident these approaches will help stimulate a steady flow of profitable work.

Business development comprises a number of techniques and responsibilities to:

1. Research new types of business, products or services with an emphasis on identifying gaps (existing and/or expected) in the mitigation of needs of potential clients (existing and/or new ones).

2. Attract new customers and penetrate existing markets.

Table of Contents

Purpose of this Handbook   v

About the Author   viii

Stairway to Heaven – A Model for How BD Works   1

The ABC of BD – Managing Your Contacts List   5

Profile-Raising – What Works and What Doesn't   9

25 Tips for Improving BD Effectiveness   15

Networking at a Reception – Who to Talk to, What to Say   19

The Basics of Selling – Credibility, Rapport and Trust   24

The Four Stages of Selling – Background, Issues, Concerns and Solutions   30

20 Killer Selling Questions   36

But What Services Should You Be Marketing?   39

Developing Client Relationships - The Sherwood Client Planning Tool   45

Latest Developments in CRM in the Professions   54

Action Planning   64

About the Author

Tony Reiss has more than 20 years experience helping partners to become more effective leaders and develop more profitable business from stronger client relationships. He is a certified Master Coach and accredited to use the MBTI psychometric indicator. He has worked with more than 30 of the top law firms and was awarded Law Firm Trainer of the Year by the LETG in 2009/10 along with colleagues Sally Woodward and Des O'Connell.

Tony studied Management Studies at Templeton College, Oxford. He has an MA from St Catherine's College, Oxford and an MPhil from Reading University.

Tony started his career marketing with Procter & Gamble. He became a senior marketing consultant with Deloitte Haskins & Sells working with the BBC, BP, BT, Prudential, Rank, Shell, and the London Stock Exchange before becoming Head of Marketing for the management consultancy.

In 1990 Tony joined Cameron Markby Hewitt (now CMS Cameron McKenna) as Marketing Director. He introduced planning processes that contributed to Camerons being the first professional firm in the City to be accredited as an Investor in People.

Before founding Sherwood, he was a Principal Tutor on the MBA in Legal Practice at the Nottingham Law School for several years.

Tony has had numerous articles published in Managing Partner, Professional Marketing, IBA's Law Firm Management Newsletter and The Law Society Gazette. He often speaks at conferences.

A further handbook on the specialist art of pitching is also available from Tony, called **Pitch Perfect**.

Contact details:

Email:tony.reiss@reiss-consulting.com

Blog: http://tonyreiss.com

Direct: +44 20 8408 2242

Mobile: +44 79 6772 6733

About Sherwood PSF Consulting

Sherwood is a leading consultancy to professional service firms all over the world. The firm was founded in 1999. Its seven principals are all lawyers or have held senior management positions in law firms, legal departments or barristers' chambers. The firm also works with a wider network of other specialists.

The expertise and experience of the principals cover the consulting and learning & development waterfront, with an emphasis on:

- supporting firms in formulating and implementing significant initiatives to change or improve their business performance.

- designing and delivering programmes and coaching partners or directors.

Stairway to Heaven – A Model for How BD Works in Law Firms

An overview of the **Prospects to Advocates** process in law firms can helpfully be illustrated by my model - 'Stairway to Heaven' – so called partly because it's one of my favourite Led Zep numbers, but also because the stairway continues upwards towards what might be called BD nirvana.

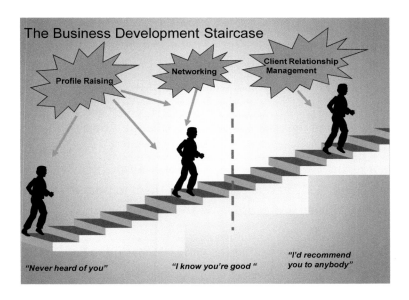

Every time Joe hears about you and your firm and hears that you're good, or is interested in what you have to say, imagine that he goes up one step.

This approach will work for a while, but it only gets you so far. You might be lucky and receive instructions simply from profile-raising activities, but more often than not you need to meet Joe first. This is what I call **networking**. You might meet Joe at a conference, perhaps talking to the person sitting next to you or talking to someone during the 'networking break', or at a seminar at your offices or a trade industry gathering.

This is your chance to engage in a useful dialogue, finding out about Joe, the company, their challenges as well as getting across a sense that you know your stuff. A chapter below goes into more detail on the art of networking. But for now, your aim can be summarised as getting Joe to say *"[You and your firm] are good. I like you and can imagine working with you."*

At this stage there's an important challenge – how to convert this goodwill into getting instructions. This is such a delicate stage that I've given the subject a separate chapter. But I'll tell you now that you don't just wait for them to phone you! You should drive this process.

For now let's assume that the work has started to flow in....

It's usually a great moment when you start to win work from a new client. There should be pats on the back, mentions in internal newsletters and a rightful feeling of achievement. But this is when the work really begins. Can you imagine what happens at the law firm that might have expected to be instructed? They'll be trying to oust you, perhaps offering the client discounted prices or offering trips to major sporting events etc. So your focus should be on **managing the client relationship**, as follows:

- Ensuring you do an outstanding job
- Using the opportunity of working with Joe to deepen your relationship
- Using the opportunity of working together to develop relationships with others in the client organisation who are buyers of legal services, or who can influence the process.

Law firms are getting better at doing this and again I offer below a separate chapter on the subject.

Your challenge when managing client relationships is not necessarily to get all their work. It's not always in the interests of clients to give all their legal work to a single firm. What if there's a conflict? What if the relationship gets too complacent? Your target instead is to get the client to say *"Wow – the service I get from [you & your firm] is way better than that I get from anybody else. I'd recommend you to anybody!"*

The focus should be on building trust with the client, eventually introducing your partners, and coordinating the services you're offering so the client sees the added value your firm is providing. This sounds easy but is harder to do in practice in most firms. Let's face it, there aren't many partners who like their work to be 'coordinated' by other partners!

Prospects to Advocates - Actions to Consider

- Get your contacts list updated

- Don't just put clients on: consider those people you knew at University or Law School – they might currently work for a rival firm, but might move to work in-house!

- Ask yourself: What proportion of my BD time is spent on profile-raising, networking and managing client relationships?

- Ask yourself: Have I got that proportion right?

The ABC of BD – Managing Your Contact List

The implication of the 'stairway to heaven' model is that partners and associates need to manage a process to move their contacts up this staircase. This isn't easy, particularly when you consider that many senior lawyers will have more than 200 contacts. More importantly, it isn't easy when you consider that it is of course a downward-moving escalator.

To demonstrate this, just consider the following situation. You meet a Joe at a seminar at your firm. You have a good conversation and find out what Joe does and who for. You even discover he used to work for a firm similar to yours and you share some experiences. He goes up two metaphorical steps in just a few minutes.

But where is Joe six months later if you don't follow up and get in touch? I'll tell you where. He can't even remember your name or which firm you were at. He might even have demoted you on the basis that you hadn't bothered to get in touch. And, to make matters worse.....he's probably gone up a rival's staircase in the meantime!

You need to see your BD efforts as a campaign – not a series of one-off conversations.

This is where our ABC priority system comes in. You can't

hope to manage say 200 contacts up the staircase and still hit your chargeable hour target. So we recommend you classify your contacts into those who are top priority, those who are second tier and finally those who are long shots so that you can direct your efforts to where you are more likely to succeed.

How do you decide which ones to be your A's? Well, two or three of them might be your biggest clients. One or two of them might be clients of other partners of the firm that you hope to cross-sell to. One or two of your top priority A's might be referrers, such as banks or accountants or surveyors (ie people who can say good things about you, thereby putting you in the frame for receiving instructions). In other words these are the contacts from whom you will have the best chance of developing new or further work. We recommend you restrict your number of A's. These activities take time and five A's is much more manageable than 10.

To move A's up the staircase, you need to commit to having four meaningful marketing connections with each of them a year - a lunch maybe or a meeting with a follow up telephone conversation. Having four such conversations means that you're getting in touch every three months or so. There is a risk that more frequent marketing can be irritating and you may appear too desperate.

B's are your second tier contacts. If you had more time for

business development they might be A's. But you don't. They need two meaningful marketing connections per year to ensure you remain in the frame.

C's frankly are going to receive the minimum effort. You'll be reminding them that you exist, sending them newsletters or e-alerts, inviting them to seminars etc.

At the end of each year, you should look at your list of A's, B's and C's. Ask yourself whether you are getting anywhere with your A's. If a key person has decided to downsize, leave their job and live in the outback, you may decide your efforts are not likely to result in any rewards. Similarly you may have heard that a rival firm has not delighted one of your B clients thereby making your offering potentially more attractive. So you might demote an A to B status and promote a B to an A. But don't change your priorities lightly. Converting prospects to advocates takes time. And it can take two to three years to win substantial streams of work. Don't give up too easily.

The process can be more powerful if it's co-ordinated across a practice group, usually by practice group heads or your BD support team. This keeps up pressure and ensures contacts aren't allowed to slip.

Please note that in no way does the ABC system suggest that any client gets an inferior service. Your C contacts will be listened to with full attention. They will receive outstanding service. It's just that in terms of increasing your workflow, you'll be focussing more effort on your A's.

Prospects to Advocates - **Actions to Consider**

- Choose your five A clients. If possible choose clients where you feel there are compatible values – this helps make the relationships sustainable (a bit like choosing a marriage partner!)

- Put together an embryonic plan for these five A clients (see below)

- Choose your 15 B clients

- Find ways to make yourself have the time to develop relationships with these clients (put reminders in your calendar, get your PA to remind you etc)

Profile-raising – What Works and What Doesn't

Very little has been written on this subject and I'm not aware that any detailed research on marketing effectiveness for law firms has been carried out. Indeed most firms aren't measuring the effect of their marketing activity despite spending substantial amounts of money on it.

Part of the problem is that firms, or individual partners or associates, aren't always clear what their marketing objectives are. For example, are they targeting new clients or trying to cross sell to clients of other parts of the firm?

Most firms use a pretty conventional approach to profile-raising and put their main efforts into using a mixture of seminars and newsletters. I think this is a mistake. Not that these techniques are inherently ineffective. But several clients say things such as "I'll go crazy if I receive yet another newsletter on Employment issues!"

Firms would benefit from being clear about their brand values to help them decide what marketing techniques they should adopt. If, for example, you want to be known as a firm that offers creative solutions to commercial problems, make your marketing more creative. I know one firm that introduced short plays using carefully briefed actors into their seminars to act out certain circumstances. Clients loved it. Another firm opened up its offices as an art gallery with professional curators, to attract particular private clients.

Monitor what your competitors do to market themselves and do the opposite or at least something different. Standing out from the crowd is a huge part of what successful marketing should be doing.

And there are so many others techniques which might help your firm be distinctive. Here are some examples of more innovative and successful campaigns to raise the profile of practice groups:

1. **A firm keen to develop its dispute resolution function**
   They developed a process for keeping litigation costs under control and invited the heads of the legal functions of several large banks to a themed lunch. At the lunch the firm got insights from the banks about litigation issues from their perspective. This impressed the potential buyers – after all, their existing lawyers hadn't raised these points. This led to several 1-1 pitches after the lunch and instructions followed from two of the banks.

2. **A firm starting up a product liability function**
   They collaborated with a small software firm to develop a diagnostic tool for assessing the risk of product liability claims for UK based manufacturers.

A number of large companies were happy for the lawyers to visit their manufacturing plants and produce a useful report. It led to the firm getting short-listed for substantial corporate work with a FTSE 350 company where there was no previous relationship.

3. **A firm keen to move from tier 2 to tier 1 in Real Estate in the directories**

The Government had recently published a green paper potentially introducing new legislation. The law firm decided to carry out a survey with a leading trade publication. They published the results and ultimately influenced the new legislation. The firm thought this was so successful they have carried out subsequent surveys and has indeed moved up the rankings.

4. **A firm wanting to develop their financial services regulation practice**

The firm decided that there were likely to be further market developments and offered a research study to an MBA student. The research findings were then used to arrange meetings with the leading companies in the market. The prospective clients were impressed with the business insights the firm had.

5. **A leading shipping firm keen to develop clear blue water between them and their rivals**

   A senior female partner set up a club for all the women executives in the industry. Hundreds of women attended events specially designed for women (eg fashion shows, talks from successful senior women in business etc). This provided wonderful opportunities for women in the firm to form relationships with women working in the industry.

6. **A firm looking to develop more referrals from overseas firms**

   They targeted the satellite offices of particular firms in their home city – the firms which they judged weren't in the market to compete locally. Only 12 firms were invited to a breakfast seminar and four attended. All four referred work to the firm within the following week. A good example of what David Maister has previously called small scale seminars.

Below is an up-to-date list of marketing techniques and my own personal views as to what typically tends to work and what doesn't, in my experience. Look out for those activities with a low score (because that's good) on cost/time and a high score on impact, such as asking clients for referrals:

Marketing Activity	Cost/ time	Impact	Comment
Brochure for firm	H	L	A necessary evil?
Brochure for product	H	M	For credibility?
Technical bulletin or newsletter	M	H	Credibility; more persuasive than brochure?
Annual review magazine	M	M	Selling too overtly?
Advertising	H	L	Not persuasive for professions?
Advertorial (ie paid space)	H	M	Article more persuasive
Sponsorship	H	L	Difficult to measure
Directories	H	L	Not used by most clients? Helpful for recruitment?
Receptions/ golf days/ watch sport	H	L	As a thank you to clients
Client lunches	M	H	Good for building relationships
Using technology (eg Extranet)	L	M	Vehicle for tailored material? Interactive good.
Social networking (blogs, LinkedIn etc)	L	M	An opportunity while so few partners using blogs?
Themed lunch (discussion topic with small group)	L/M	H	Credibility; builds relationships. External speaker as an attraction?
Industry research or surveys	H	H	Expensive, but can be useful in certain instances. Use associates to gather views?
Articles in trade journals	M	L/M	Must be well written and relevant
Press releases	L	M	Need to follow up with journalists

Marketing Activity	Cost/ time	Impact	Comment
Meeting journalists and providing briefings	L	H	Give leads and quotes; keep in touch. Doesn't suit all lawyers
In-house seminars	M	H	Credibility, builds relationships, but need to be different? Avoid 'chalk and talk'!
Speaking at conferences	L	M	Pick the good events and good speakers
Chairing a conference	L	H	Establishes you as the authority
Asking clients for referrals	L	H	Just needs courage!

Key: H=High, M=Medium, L=Low

Prospects to Advocates - Actions to Consider

- Review how your competitors raise their profile – then do something different.

- Arrange a brainstorming meeting with your partners, lawyers and support staff. Select the ideas where there is some passion from team members.

- Follow up after each profile-raising event

- Ask yourself after each event: In what other ways can we eke out any further value from more profile-raising or networking opportunities?

PROFILE RAISING

25 Tips to Improve Marketing and BD Effectiveness

Having run three different in-house BD functions and having had responsibility for delivering value, I offer these ideas for improving marketing effectiveness. Some of them are high level and others are rather more specific. Some are about getting the thinking right and others are about ways of encouraging more marketing.

The big ideas

1. Distinctive brands are better than being me-too – the stronger the brand the more your firm stands out from your rivals and the less you need to spend to promote your practice

2. Having a clear strategy in terms of what work you're trying to win from what type of clients – otherwise the marketing risks being too disparate to be effective

3. Focusing on two or three things and trying to do them well, rather than 10 things done averagely

4. Aiming high but attempt foothills before Everest – otherwise people might become despondent

5. Having your lawyers being enthusiastic about marketing makes a huge difference –it might even be more important than having the right strategy?

6. Try to find the time to arrange 1-1 meetings with clients while your firm is enjoying a high profile – the combination of profile and selling works well

7. The importance of databases – an investment early on to build a comprehensive database of contacts can save a fortune later and can help you avoid irritating clients by over-marketing and measure what works

8. Asking your clients what marketing activities work well for them – they'll be flattered and will tell you

9. Having personal marketing plans so each partner and senior lawyer knows what they should be focusing on when not doing chargeable work

10. Delighting your clients with great service is the best start for attracting more work – keep asking your client for feedback on what's working and what needs improving

11. Learning from experience and assessing benefits vs costs (including time costs) – do a review after each marketing investment

12. Senior partners leading by example in terms of marketing best practice – without this, it's hard to get others to change, because others will be watching them and copying. People do what senior partners **do** – not what they **say**!

13. The importance of planning marketing – not a big

bureaucratic process, but being clear what you are trying to achieve

14. Having campaigns rather than a series of one-off activities on completely different subjects – this way you'll get noticed as the firm that knows a lot about X

15. Squeezing the most out of marketing investments – if you speak at a seminar, use the same notes to write and publish an article

16. Internal communication of marketing successes (and failures if done sensitively) to ensure useful know-how spreads throughout the firm

17. Creating an internal culture that rewards effort and success and does not punish failure – this might help partners feel more confident to have a go!

18. Having good things said about you is much more persuasive than saying good things about yourself – how can you ensure this happens?

19. Really getting to know your clients' and prospects' businesses – "people don't care how much you know until they know you care"

20. As a general rule, avoid any heavy selling – heavy things tend to sink without trace!

Prospects to Advocates - **Some Specific BD Ideas**

21. Joint marketing initiatives with leading non-legal but related specialists (eg defamation with PR agency etc)

22. Hiring MBA students for value added projects (eg in-depth market studies that prospective clients would be interested to hear about)

23. Chairing industry trade associations, or even setting up such a body

24. The power of referrals – have you tried asking your delighted clients to mention you to others? What would make it easy for you and easy for them?

25. Train some of your more presentable and eloquent partners to be more 'journalist friendly' and be on hand to add some spice to any current legal stories. Your firm could get some great publicity

Networking at a Reception

Many lawyers seem to dread going to events where they don't know anybody. At law firm receptions, we find many of the lawyers huddled together talking to each other. Who should they go up to? What should they say? How do they leave somebody who's not very interesting? Should they ask for business cards? If so, how should they do this?

This topic is one I've been asked for more help on than any other. It's important to start by reviewing the attributes, activities and social skills of effective networkers.

Networking attributes – attitudes

I think there are a lot of misunderstandings about networking and the attributes of successful networkers. It's not about being pushy and salesey. Instead, good networkers:

- Have a real desire to help people…knowing you have to give in order to receive
- Make a sincere effort rather than keeping score
- Approach their network with a sense of urgency and obligation
- Show gratitude when someone helps them

Networking attributes – activities

If you study how good networkers behave, you'll notice that they tend to do more of the following activities:

- Build knowledge about the other individual, their business and needs
- Spend time with people
- Attend conferences, writing to others, reading
- Arrange introductions/leads
- Take action on behalf of another with the belief that the person you are helping will eventually help you
- Keep in touch with people
- Agree with colleagues a "man for man" marking system with clients – so the efforts are well spread and associates become involved at an early stage.

Networking attributes - social skills

Here is a list of the skills of a good networker:

- Being pleasant, courteous and well mannered
- Able to ask good questions and being interested in the person you are talking to – they don't talk much about themselves
- Able to really listen to what the other person says
- Being able to impress with their insights, without going over-the-top

- Able to get on with a range of different person, whilst being authentic and not coming across as fake!
- Good at making a good first impression, being relaxed, confident and enthusiastic

Below are my tips on how to behave and what to say at a reception:

Joining a group

Approach the group confidently, eyes up and scanning. Do not hover and do not interrupt rudely! Enter the group saying something like:

"Hello, do you mind if I join you, I'm [   ] from [   ]

Shake hands - look them in the eye and repeat their first name to help you remember it.

Take the pressure off by handing the conversation back to the group. Use a phrase such as:-

"Sorry, please continue - - - (stay silent)"
or
"Sorry, I interrupted - - - (stay silent)"

Don't ask a question - this puts the focus and pressure on you.

Respond to a question to you with your answer and then follow with a return question.

Introducing yourself to an individual

The approach for going up to a single person is different. It doesn't sound appropriate to say **"Hello – Do you mind if I join you!"**

Instead use a phrase such as:-

"Hello, I don't think we've met. I'm [   ] from [   ]"

Shake hands. This works well – unless you have met them before and you've forgotten!

Coming across as an interesting person

When someone asks you what you do, describe your role by including some brief stories as examples. This usually animates you and helps you come across as interesting and confident.

Finding out about them

Ask questions about their role and especially examples of current issues they are addressing.

Eg *"I see you work for [   ]. What do you do for them?*

Then move on to find out more about them

Eg. *"What's it like working in Paris?"*

Exiting a conversation

If in a group situation, a simple *"excuse me"* is fine. Don't endlessly try to justify why you have to go. You don't need to knock back your glass of wine! There is no necessity to shake hands, since this disrupts the conversation.

If conversing with only one other, never leave them on their own by excusing yourself. Open your body language to the room to attract another person. If this fails, take them with you to the bar, the food or wherever to meet someone else. Do an introduction as described above then, after a couple of minutes, exit politely with a simple "excuse me".

Business cards

Make sure you have some but avoid spraying them around as if you're desperate for work. It can be better to ask for their card first and offer one of yours in return. Try to avoid the problem of mixing up other people's cards with your cards.

The Basics of Selling - Credibility, Rapport and Trust

I've asked hundreds lawyers over the years how they establish their credibility, build rapport and trusted relationships with clients and colleagues. My reason for doing this is that these skills are the foundations of building a sustainable practice.

Four Ways to Establish Credibility

Right from the word go others will form a sense as to how credible you are. Have you been there, done it and got the tee-shirt? Are you worth whatever you're charging? Do you engender a feeling of confidence in the client?

Clients might change their mind, but they'll start to see you either through rosy glasses or grey ones!

This is how professionals best establish their credibility:

- **They look the part**. I suppose this is a fairly obvious point. A client expects their professional advisor to have a certain look. It gets a bit trickier when you're working in certain sectors though. How do senior executives at Microsoft expect their lawyers to look? What about Shell, Disney, the Government? The trick is to be professional but in rapport with your client (see below).

- **They are well prepared** – so you know what you're talking about in meetings or on conference calls. Though, I'm often surprised how often associates go into meetings unbriefed in terms of who is attending and the purpose of the meeting.

- **They talk about their experience in a relevant way (not in a show-off way!)** – again an obvious way to establish credibility. Though there are dangers if you talk about your experience too much - it can have the opposite effect. A more subtle and effective approach is to use your experience to ask insightful questions.

- **They look confident, but not too much**. Some professionals underestimate how important this point is.

  A good starting point:
  - Holding good eye contact
  - Speaking with a strong voice and not too fast
  - Being able to hold silences comfortably
  - Avoiding nervous ticks
  - Having a strong authoritative posture when standing or sitting

Four Ways to Build Rapport

Clients will typically have a choice of firms who could do the work. Similarly, it rarely happens that you're the only person in the firm that could do it, so partners can choose who to give the work to.

People tend to select lawyers based more on rapport than credibility. Who do they think is on their wavelength? Who respects their values? Who will be easier and possibly more fun to work with? They might not think this through consciously but, believe me, the answers to these questions underpin their decision.

This is how professionals build rapport well:

- **They get to know their clients.** They are interested in their clients as people. They might open up a little bit about themselves to encourage an open relationship. They ask appropriate questions.

- **They demonstrate to their clients that they care and listen.** Being a good listener is key, but it's more important to demonstrate that you're a good listener. They do this by reflecting back what the client has said, by saying something like this: "So what you're saying is that X, Y and Z are all important to you". They might go further and probe to find out more, by saying something such as: "Can you say a bit more about why that's important to you?"

- **They acknowledge what their clients say and empathise.** Not only do they hear the words, but those good at rapport pick up the emotions and reflect these back. It is important to do this genuinely and not to be condescending. Something like "I can see that must have been a frustrating situation for you...." can work well.

- **They have an approach which is respectful.** There will be times when we might be tempted to feel aggrieved (eg having to work over the weekend, repeat work, do boring repetitive work etc). Those who are successful at building rapport tend to park any feelings of disappointment or frustration and get on with the work in a positive manner!

Four Ways to Develop a Trusted Relationship

If credibility can be established pretty quickly and rapport can start to be established in early meetings, trust takes much longer. You can lose trust pretty quickly and it's hard to earn it.

This is how professionals develop trusted relationships over time:

- **They deliver what and when they said they would deliver**. It is very difficult to be trusted if you promise one thing and deliver another. In today's more competitive markets, the temptation is there to over promise. To be trusted we need to deliver, not just once, but time and again.

- **They work at the highest levels of integrity and honesty**. There is a consistency between what they say and what they do and they are consistent with their messages to different groups of people. They might point out if they have little experience in one aspect of a transaction or if something hasn't gone smoothly on a transaction. The Japanese have a saying which translates as 'A Defect is a Treasure'. The way you deal with problems will influence the extent that you are trusted.

- **They respect confidentiality**. It is hard to be trusted if we reveal information that might have been communicated in confidence. It is harder than it sounds to get this right, because we might not always be aware of what is sensitive information.

- **They put their client's interests level with their own.** Many clients feel that their professional advisors are trying to maximise their chargeable hours. This is hardly going to engender a spirit of trust. If as an advisor you can be looking to give your clients the best possible value, a greater feeling a trust will develop.

All of us can improve our skills in establishing credibility, rapport and trust. An interesting couple of questions to ask yourself:

- Are you generally better at establishing credibility, building rapport or establishing trusted relationships?
- What could you do to develop your skills?

The Four Stages of Selling – Background, Issues, Concerns, Solutions

BICS is a simple acronym that was devised by Sherwood as a reminder of the four stages of the sales process. BICS stands for **Background**, **Issues**, **Concerns**, **Solutions**. It is a simple model and is intended to be a checklist or guideline for selling, presenting four steps in a logical sequence of events. It can be used with both existing and prospective clients to develop the relationship by gaining information, generating engagement and ultimately winning new business.

In basic terms, once we have built a relationship, clients will become more comfortable to open up about their issues and will listen to you offering your thoughts and ultimately trust you to help with a solution. If the solution matches the client needs, they are prompted or stimulated to overcome their natural caution and may then become motivated to take action.

Throughout this entire process you should be aiming to communicate that you are **credible**, in **rapport** with their values and someone that can be totally **trusted**, as discussed above.

Background

Imagine meeting a new potential client whilst having a coffee break at a seminar. What should you talk about? You would obviously want to create an immediate impact and make a positive first impression. This helps them to warm to you and will enable you to establish a rapport.

Do your research beforehand whenever possible. Try to get a list of who might be attending any event. Choose a small number of people you'd ideally want to meet. Spend some time preparing by reading up about their company, about them and about issues in their sector. Ideally find a handful of relevant topics to talk about to each of them.

Do not even think about selling, as selling prematurely turns people off, undermines how much you'll be trusted and can close the door on any further conversations. Your goal should be to build a relationship. It's a bit like dating. Wooing works better than looking for marriage partners straight away!

Good openers can be exclamations or opinions followed by 'what is your view on this'?

Other examples of useful conversation openers are:

- What did you find interesting about …?
- Have you noticed…?

Bad openers fail to provide an opportunity to develop the relationship and give them something to object to or just bore them - such as:

- I've got just the thing you want...
- I'd like to arrange to meet you so that I might...

Avoid words like "I", "me", "we", "our firm", etc. as much as possible. The word "you" should feature more prominently.

Issues

Imagine now that you meet this contact on a subsequent occasion. You will notice that the conversation should feel easier and more natural. You start this conversation knowing a bit about each other. Once you are in the discussion, you will have an opportunity to move the relationship on. You can do this by:

- Showing that you listened to what they talked about last time
- Asking about what they are working on
- Probing to ascertain their challenges and issues
- Telling them things which may be interesting or useful to them (eg developments in legislation or jurisdictions they are interested in etc)
- Demonstrating similar experiences to show you are in rapport and empathising
- Engaging them and getting them actively involved

THE FOUR STAGES OF SELLING

Be aware of their reactions and behaviour and adapt. Listen as much with your eyes as your ears. People give clues when they are interested and engaged and also when they are bored!

Keep your questions open-ended where possible. Remember, these need to be relevant and tailored. Always think about the purpose of your discussion.

Concerns

We all live with issues! We may accept that things aren't perfect but we often don't do anything about them. On something as big as instructing a new law firm we need to be motivated at a level of at least nine out of ten to take the necessary action. This stage of the selling process is about adding this level of motivation.

You will often get signals from the client that they are ready to move to this stage. They might ask, for example, about how something might work or what might go wrong. You might have to take the lead and suggest a meeting based on something they said at a previous meeting. For example:

"You mentioned last time that you are considering moving the business in Central & Eastern Europe. We have a good deal of experience in that region and would be happy to share some tips. There are several commonly held misconceptions etc"

Consider why the client should buy your services? Most people will buy because they are looking for solutions to pressing business problems, additional resources to close gaps or the means to cope with difficult issues. Or there might be more personal benefits. For example, making the buyer's life easier or helping them look good in their organisation.

This is fundamental buying psychology. If you can't address any of these issues in a meeting, it is unlikely that you will be able to generate sufficient interest for a second round. Remember that your clients or prospects will be evaluating you on three principal factors:

- *Credibility*: do they exude a quiet confidence that they can deliver?
- *Rapport*: do they really care and understand us and me in particular?
- *Trust*: will they put our interests right up there and bust a gut to deliver value?

Once they are interested in you and what you have to say, continue to explore and investigate, build trust and rapport. Identify and agree client needs, priorities and constraints on both a personal and organisation level. Remove any feelings of doubt about you, your integrity or ability and present yourself with credibility and enthusiasm.

Once you have raised their awareness of the benefits of taking action or the risks to them and their business if they don't, they will be motivated to act......

Solutions

Assuming everything has been covered and that you have listened to their needs and provided evidence that you will deliver, this stage should be relatively straightforward.

If some issues and concerns haven't been covered, you'll get objections to proceeding and these will need to be uncovered and explored.

During your conversation, watch out for the signals the client is sending. Summarise your conversation and deal with any issues or concerns which may have arisen. Gain their commitment on appropriate action and close the conversation by agreeing the action. For example:

"I'd like to provide you with a fee quote. When are you free to meet to discuss your precise requirements on the new development project? When would suit you best?"

20 Killer Selling Questions

Selling doesn't work if you simply go through a list of pre-prepared questions. There is no equivalent McDonald's formula for making the perfect hamburger! It works much better if you tune in carefully to what the prospect says and ask follow up probing questions and summarise frequently, like this.

1.   *It sounds to me from what you're saying that x,y, z are all important to you. Is that right? Can you say more about that?*

The more you have invested in building a good relationship and established your credibility, rapport and trust, the more incisive and probing your questions can be. Here is a list of other killer questions that might be useful to cover:

2.   *What proportion of your legal work is catered in-house and how much is outsourced to external law firms?* Follow up their answer with:

3.   *Tell me more about why you operate in this way?*

4.   *What do you look for in external law firms?* Prompts will help establish what is more important to them: fees (competitive/discounted/capped); legal advice; innovative solutions; added value services such as training/knowledge-sharing and research services?).

Follow up their answer with:

5.   ***Tell me more about why those services are important to you?***

6.   ***How do you like to work with external law firms?*** Very important question to establish preferred working practices: how many touch-points do they want with a law firm, do they have large teams, who are their internal clients, do they want the relationship to be built vertically (i.e. only top people) or horizontally (i.e. across all levels of the organisation), what level of communication do they like/need? Again, follow up their answer with:

7.   ***Tell me more about why that kind of relationship is important to you?***

8.   ***What are your business priorities at the moment, for the next 6 months, 12 months?***

9.   ***In which jurisdictions?***

10. ***What projects are you currently working on?***

11. ***Tell us more about the timeframe for these projects?***

12. ***How might you use external counsel to support you on this?***

13. ***When will you be appointing external counsel?***

14. ***What might we need to do to put ourselves in the frame for being appointed?***

Here is a list of questions that might be specifically related to being appointed to law firm panels:

15. *What sort of law firm panel arrangements do you currently have in place?*

16. *Who is responsible for your law firm panel review?*

17. *How many law firms do you have on your panel?*

18. *Which law firms are currently on your panel?*

19. *Tell us about the process you use to review your panel and the frequency of panel reviews?*

20. *What would be the process for us to be considered for your law firm panel?*

But What Services Should You Be Marketing?

So far we've looked at how business development works (our stairway to heaven), the importance of having priorities (ABC lists) and the effectiveness of various techniques for profile-raising. We haven't actually yet looked at what services you should be marketing.....until now.

This is usually one of the first things I work on with my coaching clients. Some partners have a well defined practice in that they have focused on doing one type of work for one type of client (eg regulatory work for companies in the aviation market, or trademark work for companies with substantial brand portfolios or acquisition finance for banks etc). Other partners are struggling with their marketing because they have too general a practice. They might be a commercial litigator or do general corporate M&A type work.

I have developed a simple yet effective way of establishing what services each partner should focus on. The process enables partners to develop a personal strategy which involves matching two things:

- Your 'marketable assets' (ie What areas you are good at and motivated by)
- The areas of the market that are profitable, have

growth potential and which connect with other areas the firm is interested in.

How to establish your marketable assets

I start by asking the partner to obtain a list of matters they've been involved with over the last three to five years. It's amazing how many matters we forget about!

There are then three zones to focus on:

- Knowledge/experience
- Skills/capabilities/strengths
- Network of contacts (inside and outside the firm)

And there are two questions in each zone:

- Define your particular strengths/capabilities
- Define what could be added to your strengths to make you significantly more marketable

The diagram below shows how the questions relate to the three zones.

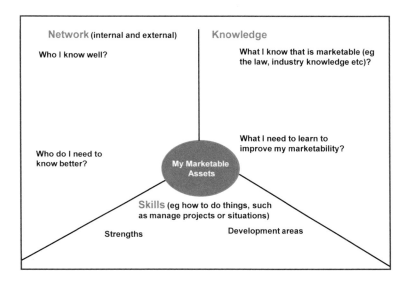

Then we have to analyse the opportunities in the marketplace. You don't have to have lots of data and spend ages doing research. Any partner that has been working in their field for at least two or three years should know this stuff intuitively. The proforma for analysing the market is below:

The process is relatively straightforward:

- List the types of work and types of client you've acted for over recent years
- Describe the size, growth trends and profitability of that market or type of work by grading them High, Medium or Low
- Then describe to what extent there might be

synergies with other parts of the firm (the more connections, the better since it is unlikely your career will flourish if your practice is like an island floating off the mainland!)

- Now link to the analysis you've done on 'My Marketable Assets' to cross check that you're the right person for the job
- Finally, consider to what extent you really love doing that kind of work for those kinds of clients. This, in my experience is probably the single most important factor to determine whether you will have a thriving career.

The output from this analysis should ideally provide a focus for your marketing. There might be one main type of work you want to do, which is based on experience you already have and represents a profitable opportunity to the firm. There might also be a sector to focus on.

I coached one partner and used these tools. He had a broad practice in a technology group. We settled on outsourcing as the type of work and retailing as an attractive sector.

Another partner, who was a litigator, built his career by developing his reputation in IT and document management.

I want to take this opportunity to underline the increasing importance of lawyers having a sector focus. Clients will like you more if you understand their world and their language. Try being credible in the IT sector if you don't know your bits from your bytes!

Market Analysis to Establish Marketing Priorities

Sector/Products	Size of Market	Growth of Market	Profitability of Work	Attractiveness to the Firm	My Experience	Level of Passion
Describe **client types** (eg investment banks, retail etc) Describe **types of work** (eg M&A, IP, financing, etc)	H,M,L	H,M,L	H,M,L	Describe 'fit' with the firm and other firm initiatives. Consideration of competitor offerings.	Describe in what way you have valuable experience, skills or a useful network (refer to 'my marketable assets' analysis)	H,M,L

Planning to Develop Client Relationships (or leaving it to serendipity?)

Client relationships might improve if you leave things to chance. But they're much more likely to improve if you stop and think about the relationship and plan your approach more systematically.

I'm often shocked at how little partners and senior associates know about their clients, particularly the client's business objectives. I'm also disappointed how little planning goes into having a lunch with a client or prospect.

I recommend spending at least an hour preparing before a lunch to ensure you've updated yourself on recent events. They may have launched a new product or expanded into a new country. There may be something in a trade magazine about a licensing dispute with a contractor. There may have been redundancies. One of their competitors may have done something novel. Ideally you should have an informal agenda with five potentially fruitful conversations.

Once you've gained sufficient insight into the client, I recommend producing a Client Relationship Plan. It can be updated every now and again, but the key thing is having a dedicated team of partners and associates to coordinate developing the relationship.

I recommend having regular and frequent meetings just to talk about the client relationship. One firm I've worked with had short (around 15 mins) weekly meetings so the Client Partner could get an update on matters and ensure relationships were progressing.

If you're interested to see the Sherwood proforma for a Client Relationship Plan, see below:

©The Sherwood Client Planning Tool

1. Overview and update on the client's business

- overall state of the business, client's competitive position within its market(s)

- growing and declining sectors of business

- recent client business developments (acquisitions, mergers)

- likely future strategy

2. Use of legal services

- overall policies on retention of an in-house team/ instructing and using external law firms (centralised, decentralised)

- the client's policies on pricing, conflicts, documentation etc,

- favoured selection criteria (price, expertise, personal contact etc.)

- law firms primarily used for particular services / business groups / countries.

3. Client's key personnel

- heads of operating units

- legal department(s)

- reporting lines

- analysis of the firm's relationship with the key individuals at all levels

4. The client relationship

- the historic development of the relationship, key milestones

- significant recent matters

- competitive position re other law firms

- 3 - year billing history (draw out key factors such as large one-off jobs which may distort overall billing trends)

5. The firm's client team

- composition and responsibilities

- recent client relationship building activities (secondments, seminars, client entertainment etc.)

6. Strategy for developing the client relationship

short and medium term goals e.g.

- develop / defend the relationship in certain client business areas / geographic regions

- develop the firm's relationship with identified key executives

- expand the core client team / widen client team as appropriate

- pricing policies (discounts on certain work, volume based pricing arrangement etc.)

7. Action plan

- communication with the client on active matters/ billings/conflicts

- communication on aspects of the relationship (review meetings, client contact cards etc.)

- future secondments (to legal departments or business groups)

- keeping the client team up to date (meetings, email lists, internal bulletins etc.)

- targeting of publications, seminar invitations, client entertainment etc.

- client team responsibilities

Action	Responsible	Timing

Latest Developments in CRM in the Professions

The advertisement from a global law firm in The Economist magazine grabbed my attention. Under a colour photograph of an archetypal psychologist's couch, the headline read "TELL ME ABOUT THE RELATIONSHIP WITH YOUR LAWYER". The copy continued….."It turns out, there was no relationship…."

The reality is that many professional service firms are finding it difficult to replicate the customer relationship management (CRM) successes achieved by service providers in other markets. So I thought firms might find it helpful to have a fresh look at what the critical success factors are.

The Research Details

What follows is based on two CRM projects I've worked on recently and some interviews I've conducted with other professional organisations, as follows:

- two top twenty law firms, widely judged to be pioneers in CRM
- two big 4 accounting firm, which have had more than 20 years running international CRM programmes
- two not-for-profit bodies providing qualifications and training to the professional sector

- an international manufacturer of food products which needs to build close relationships within the grocery sector.

This last one might look odd! I have included it because I believe this more sophisticated and competitive market could offer insights for professional firms.

The findings were as follows and I discuss them below:

- **Choose the right clients**
- **Get to the top**
- **It's the relationship not the sale**
- **It takes training and practice**
- **Making it happen**

Choose the right clients

The biggest clients won't necessarily be the best clients, though they obviously need to offer good potential. The most important aspect for choosing the right clients is that you have a similar set of values and are in 'rapport' with them. This means that the extra effort you put in is more likely to lead to rewards.

The other finding is that CRM seems to work better when the efforts are channelled on fewer clients. The grocery manufacturer put it this way:

*Working out which customers we should put particular emphasis on was key to our success. We discovered that it wasn't necessarily the biggest customers. **We had to see signs that we were compatible**. We developed a couple of tests. One involved mapping the current relationship. The other analysed the potential in the relationship.*

One of the law firms added:

Some of our best successes have been where our partners, frankly, just hit it off with the client! The other thing we discovered was that we were trying to develop relationships with too many clients. When we cut the list down, we could provide more support and things improved.

Get to the top

Once you've selected the right clients, find out what they are trying to do with their business. What is their vision? How are they proposing to get there? What support are they looking for from their professional advisors? What gets up their noses? Without this knowledge it will be difficult to manage the relationship in ways that will support their vision.

The Relationship Partner might be the right person to have this meeting. An alternative would be to invite a more senior representative from the firm (eg senior partner) to meet their counterpart. It might depend on who it is important to meet from the client side.

An additional benefit of top-to-top meetings is that they show real commitment to building a relationship. As seen by the grocery manufacturer:

> Top-to top meetings also helped us demonstrate our commitment to building the relationship and this helped give the relationship some momentum

Where there is currently a limited relationship with, say, the Board of the client, one of the big 4 accounting firms has found it useful to offer clients useful insights on sector business issues that might provide competitive advantage:

> We find 'thought leadership' programmes work well for us. We might research an industry issue and use this to help us open doors. We have realised that to impress clients, it's important to be clear what your value proposition is. How will you help your clients? We typically spend hours preparing for top-to-top meetings to ensure we get our agenda and insights correct.

For other clients, perhaps where more transactional work is already underway, the top-to-top meeting might focus on a service review to uncover what aspects of service were going well and what needs to be improved.

But how do you measure relationships, I hear you wonder! A big 4 firm uses a checklist and point system:

> We use a 10 point scale. If we haven't met them and we don't think they have heard of us, we're at ground zero. If we've met, they know what we do and think we're good, we'd score them 5 or 6. When they instruct us, it moves them up to 7. Only if they recommend us to others do they score 10.

A law firm provides a prompt sheet with their client relationship teams to help them consider ways of getting to know their client contacts:

> To encourage our partners to get to know their clients better we have given them a list of areas to explore, including their careers, interests outside work, ambitions, hopes and fears, how their bonus is comprised etc. Some of these topics are safer to talk about than others. Our partners obviously need to build more trusted relationships to comfortably talk about some of the deeper stuff.

Most partners find these sorts of conversation uncomfortable, so this brings me on to the next insight....

It takes training and practice

It's easy suggesting that partners should build closer relationships with clients. It's much harder in practice and firms are starting to address this by providing training and coaching in relationship-building. An important aspect in such training is skills practice (otherwise known by that dreaded word 'role-play'!).

Training can be designed to help answer questions such as:

- How do you pick up the phone and arrange to meet a senior member of the client team who you hardly know?
- What are the best ways of winning work from our rival firm?
- How do you get the associates and your PA to play an increasing role in developing relationships with clients?

One of the big 4 accounting firms has utilised their PA's in their CRM programme:

> I'm not sure how good we are at motivating the back office in our CRM programme. This is an area we need to look at further, though we have recognised some talented PA's/secretaries. So we launched a PA programme. This involves our PA's meeting client PA's.

They might have drinks or attend any of our sponsorship events. This has helped improve client relationships enormously. It's like it's oiled the wheels.

One of the professional bodies has used CRM training throughout their organisation.

It's made a big difference to have the skills training linked to the Relationship Management project. Our Directors and Heads have all praised the top-to-top training and we're now training our Director PA's.

One of the law firms added:

We could probably do more to engage with the support staff who deal with our key clients – I accept that our service is only as good as the weakest link

Another law firm added:

We are having great success offering partners and senior associates one-to-one coaching on BD and developing client relationships particularly at important stages of their careers.

Making it happen

The firms making most progress with CRM seem to put the

most emphasis on making things happen, rather than just talking about it.

One of the law firms said:

> *Out of our top 20 clients, the ones that work best seem to meet most often (some meet weekly for just 10-15 minutes) and chase people to ensure actions are implemented. Support from the BD function is important. We attend meetings and provided checklists for client team meetings and proforma relationship plans. These help give team meetings a focus.*

The grocery manufacturer put more emphasis on joint business plans with the customer and ensuring the customer could see early results:

> *Drafting a joint business plan with the customer is important. Without the customer involvement we felt we wouldn't get their commitment. We also put great emphasis on good quality execution. We were aware that little things could spoil the effect of what we were trying to do. We felt it was important to hold monthly meetings to progress the plan and track performance to demonstrate results.*

The joint business plan is interesting. It implies that a conversation has been held where the supplier says that the client is strategically important to them. How many professional firms say this to their client? Producing a plan to develop a client relationship will probably be helpful. Producing, with the client, a plan to add value to both parties is on a different level of commitment and lead to great results. One of the professional bodies used a relatively sophisticated contact management system. This enabled them to monitor client contacts and produce a report based on a 'traffic light' code, in which no contact over a 3 month period might produce a 'red alert'.

> We have a powerful database in which every interaction with a key organisation is recorded. The database is hugely important to us because our relationships are complex. It's like a big matrix. Everybody is encouraged to contact who they know, regardless of who the Relationship Manager is. We call it a "web of contacts". They just have to tell the Relationship Manager the outcome.

Conclusion

There are, of course, many systemic challenges in professional service firms with respect to CRM, namely:

- Partners are typically more comfortable with the task of doing their technical work and less comfortable with building client relationships

- The measurement and reward processes used by many professional firms do not encourage the behaviours associated with good CRM, eg:
  - spending time deepening and broadening client relationships, or
  - introducing other partners to their contacts.

The long term breakthroughs will probably be achieved by addressing these fundamental issues. Meanwhile, I hope you find some of the insights in this research useful.

Action Planning: Prospects to Advocates: So what? Now what?

1. **What would you like to do differently as a result of reading *Prospects to Advocates* ?**

2. **What actions will you take to make this happen? Identify specific situations.**

3. **What challenges do you foresee?**

4. **What support will you need? How will you ensure you get it?**

BV - #0057 - 190821 - C74 - 210/148/3 - PB - 9780755213993 - Gloss Lamination